# Scattered Dreams

Christy A. Weber

BookLeaf
Publishing

India | USA | UK

Presentation by *BookLeaf Publishing*

Web: www.bookleafpub.com

E-mail: info@bookleafpub.com

ISBN: 9789363311862

First edition 2024

*Dedicated to my mother, Robin Weber.*

# ACKNOWLEDGEMENT

I offer many thanks to my sisters, Beth Patterson and Audrey Yoeckel, and my brother Richard Weber, who all loved being creative and always showed me how fun it was regardless of the outcome. Thanks to my Aunt Elaine Culver, and my niece J. R. Turner, who always encouraged me in all my endeavors. Thanks to my cousin Lori Weber who kept me going through both good times and hard times. Most of all, thanks to my parents, Russ and Robin Weber, for being creative individuals who took the steps to achieve their dreams, which is such a wonderful legacy. There are so many more artists, writers and creative individuals including my family and friends who continue to inspire me in a variety of ways. I am blessed, indeed. Thank you to the editors and cover designer who made me proud of this book you are reading. Finally, to you, dear reader, thank you for reading this book. I hope you find something of yourself in these poems. I hope you find a poem you love. I hope you are inspired to express yourself.

# I DREAMT OF FERLINGHETTI

I dreamt of Ferlinghetti
Having tea with Rabbie Burns,
While Milton, Donne, and Mr. Keats
All were taking turns
Being mother with the teapot
When in walked Mr. Nash
With Dickinson and Angelou
And plates of corned beef hash.
Plath and Sexton sat together
Smoking cigarettes,
Staring at their own reflections
Speaking of regrets.
Hughes and Frost sang harmony
With a parrot in a cage.
Neruda bit each onion
Which put Ginsberg in a rage.
All were meant to come together,
To create a masterpiece;
Perhaps a sonnet, or pantoum,
But inspiration ceased.
While the Brownings danced the Tarantella,
I heard dear Rabbie say,
"I think we'll need a double dram
To write a poem today"!

# WHEN IN FLOWS
# THE TIDE

Lo, the magic and the wonder
of this sweet circadian ride.
Night and day do both obey
when in flows the tide.
Out it goes to send you forth
to that dorsal edge of space,
where Jove and Hera do doth dwell
And Morpheus gives chase.

# ALONG  THE RIVER

Shimmering aspens
Straight and tall with bright white trunks
Golden Sentinels
Standing at the water's edge
Leaves waving the river on.

# T1M3 CH4N635
# & OTHER TITLES

*"I know someday you'll have a beautiful life, I*
*know you'll be a star, in somebody else's sky but*
*why can't it be mine?"* —
*Black / Pearl Jam, 1992*


Remembering this broken mixtape
the one you labeled:
    T1M3 CH4N635
in leet, because you thought it was cool.

You made it in the winter of '97
when we came back to Texas
the cassette worn now & yellowed
with some missing gear teeth
but well played for many years
last found in a dusty box of odd mementos
the Maxell case, long gone.

you added "The Perfect Drug"
by Nine Inch Nails
 — saying it was romantic
& Brainiacs' "Fresh New Eyes"
 — saying it was deep

just for fun or so you said,
 for a bit more of the B's,
 — you added Beck & Blur
& Blind Melon & The Breeders

with other bullets from your arsenal,
you filled up both sides
yet it was "Black" by Pearl Jam
that you loved and sang along to
so fearlessly in your best Eddie Vedder voice.

you added it last & I saw you last
in the last days of the last century
while you became a mere shimmer of memories
among scattered dreams
proving once again
that times change
& time changes everything
& I wonder what kind of mixtape
you would make for me today.

# FIBONACCI FORMED

Dreams
Sparks
Gaining
Momentum
A voracious force
Firing through synaptic gaps
Neurons swiftly transmitting toward methods
of lexis

# NOCTURNAL FANTASIA

In the magical, mystical night of dreams,
There comes unheard, unseen,
From places no one's ever known,
Where no mortal has ever been.

Wee, elfin creatures with angel wings,
White stallions? Who's to say.
Like Pegasus in a moon-drenched night,
All agleam, they play.

They gambol and prance
the whole night through,
While darkness is about,
But Oberon leads them
to their sweet rest
Before the sun comes out.

Perchance, one night while Morpheus reigns,
They'll come into your dream.
For that's the only place these sprites,
By mortals, can be seen.

# UPON VIEWING MATISSE'S "WOMAN IN A PURPLE COAT"

Lydia, his model, is staring at us.
Lounging languid yet alert,
Open and confident.
All nestled on her chaise
In calm and quiet repose.

Yet the image is flat and linear
With no shading or shadow
Like a drafted dream,
Or a child's drawing,
Yet vibrant with color.

Oh the colors!
Her clothing and décor
So bold and bright and lively
With fluid lines of texture,
Expressing definition
Of floor, walls, and fabric.

And her little table,
Topped with flowers in a vase,
And pieces of fruit.

Even her purple coat

Her lovely purple coat, her robe
A shade of violet, outlined in black
With white lines of pattern
Running through the purple.

Yet her hands – they appear unfinished,
Untended. Like a mere afterthought.
Incidental of the art. Lineless.

How easily this impression,
This expression,
could become an abstraction.
If not for Lydia,

As she sits staring out at us.
Lounging languid yet alert,
Open and confident.
All nestled on her chaise
In calm and quiet repose.

# UPON VIEWING BERNINI'S APOLLO AND DAPHNE

The way you shape marble,
Did you shape it like clay,
All soft in your hands?
Was it really the strike
Of hammer and chisel
Against the cold hard stone
That formed the grooves and lines?
How did you bring about such a vision?
How did you turn marble into butter?
So full of motion and emotion
The pursuit and the metamorphosis
The billowing and curling of the cloth,
The details of the faces
And the changing body,
Their story is told in a frozen moment
Created for us centuries ago.
While here I now stand, amazed.

# THERE ONCE WAS A MIGHTY KING OF SPAIN

There once was a mighty King of Spain
Who while at night so still he lain
Had dreamt of all the many triumphs
His future held to claim

He dreamt of glories, richness pure
Of accolades and acclaims
His people on him would bestow
Vast fortune and much fame

The sun-kissed skies of Barcelona
The winding streets of Seville
The beautiful hills of Madrid too
All gave the King a thrill

To think of this glorious kingdom
And the wonderful people within
Recipients of his awesome grace
Beloved as like kin.

And yet the king within him knew
The reality of his life
When he awoke he wiped his eyes
And glanced upon his wife

He sighed and wished that all were true
He wished his wife was but a queen
Yet he was just a working man
And this was just a dream.

# ONE MORE TIME

One more time
we could sit together
in the café down the street
sipping our hazelnut cappuccinos,
speaking of teddy bears and casinos,
planning places to visit nearby
to spy the formation of clouds in the sky
over the breaking waters of Lake Michigan,
And taking photos of blooming flowers,
while stopping later for happy hour,
if only we could do this
one more time.

# ON THE WAY TO MACHYNLLETH

A gentle mist enshrouds the mountain,
as flowing water makes quiet conversation
among the river rocks.
The moon has yet to meet the sun
upon this place.
A bird soars on its wing
in the flight of dreams.
While I, the intruder, am only here.

# ONLY TIME WILL TELL

You no longer come around to visit
Are you just living your life? I must know.
Is something wrong? What happened?
What is it?
Are you even alive? I worry so.

You know I was there the day you were born.
You know I've loved you your whole life long.
Was it something I said, or did? I'm torn.
Are you homeless, or hurt, or worse,
What's wrong?

Your father's gone, he was younger than you.
After all these years, I still feel that grief.
You've been gone so long, have I lost you too?
In life, I've learned that death is a thief.

My hope is that you are happy and well.
Will you come back? Only time will tell.

# ADOPTED OPINIONS

We trade in the currency
of other people's thoughts

Now in this world, how shaky
our standards of excellence are

Ego reigns polarized, while right & wrong
are widely and wildly discussed

We speak out fervently
with those newly adopted opinions

Yet never dare to risk any
compassion or tolerance at all

# FRESHLY SERVED

Your words
  found
on my platter
so freshly served
  medium rare
on the verge of being
  raw
with sides of buttered
  adjectives
and hot-baked
  verbs
I cut into them
  chewing
thoughtfully
lost in moments
  of time
for you've tried
to keep them
  tender
yet I choke
on a bit of found
  gristle
chewing & wondering
if you expect me to
  swallow it all

# MOOD SIGNS

The smell of alcohol on your breath
in your wild turkey stupor
is shrill, like a whistle
signaling into my ear
cautioning an attack of romance
or the foreplay of aggression
so, I push you away, checking
your mood for signs of love
or anger or exhaustion
and I lead you
into the kitchen to feed you
eggs and pancakes
hoping that you and your mood will be
too tired then for anything
but the lull of dreams

# TELL ME WHAT HAPPENED

We vowed to love till death do us part.
When was it that your love began to fade?
Tell me what happened. How did it start?
We vowed to love till death do us part.
Then soon you showed me your hardening heart.
Was this your great plan, or was it fate?
We vowed to love till death do us part.
When was it that your love began to fade?

# TEARS - a pantoum

Tears flowed from my eyes as I was crying.
Crying hard from the onion's scent.
All the while, I was certainly trying
to stop the tears the onion's scent had sent.

Crying hard from the onion's scent,
I strained to see where pieces had been flying.
To stop the tears the onion's scent had sent,
I ate some bread — I heard that stops the crying.

I strained to see where pieces had been flying.
My cutting board is littered with confetti.
I ate some bread — I heard that stops the crying
I should just buy the sauce for my spaghetti.

My cutting board is littered with confetti.
The garlic is gone, I wonder where it went?
I should just buy the sauce for my spaghetti.
To cut and make a dent within the scent.

The garlic is gone. I wonder where it went?
All the while I was certainly trying
To cut and make a dent within the scent,
Those tears flowed from my eyes; I was crying.

# THE SALT LICK

So she licks the salty rim of her glass
just before sipping her Margarita
this dear is looking like a Lolita
teasing and full of innocence and sass
taking delight in the drink in her glass
she's a happy hour señorita
as she licks the salt.
Yet truly, she is no innocent lass
forty-four and still a fair bonita
she'd rather just have her Margarita
expressing her joy in moments that pass
while she licks the salt.

# HOW TO BE A FIRE-BREATHING DRAGON

To be a fire-breathing dragon
All flush with the oxymoron of
 sweet sweat
And the rub of
 toxic heat,
Just pass the
 chili con carne
Made with hot
 dragon's breath peppers
Through your open mouth
onto your poor, unsuspecting tongue!
Then you will see
 you will be
A fire-breathing dragon!

# DREAMS OF CHOCOLATE

Opening all cupboards and drawers
searching for those
semi-sweet
morsels of chocolate untouched
just to feed this need

Taking out the round box of oats
only to find a forgotten bag
of raisins, hard and stuck together
no morsels at all

Hard raisins
such a sad excuse
for my treat
when my heart
was set on chocolate morsels
silky velvet and sweet

Accepting my failure
to feed my need
these raisins
will have to do instead
for my dreams of chocolate.

# FAMILY BBQ
# AT UNCLE DICK'S

Smitty played us a lively tune.
His squeeze box rested on his lap,
Back and forth his fingers would tap.

Buster too would be playing soon.
Strumming his guitar and joining in.
A melody to stir us kin.

Dick started the grill before noon.
Smoking brisket, ribs, and chicken.
Making sauce from his own kitchen.

Mavis brought out dishes of food.
To the patio while shooing flies,
With salad, cornbread, beans, and pies.

We were joyous those afternoons.
With bellies full and singing songs,
Days like this made our hearts belong.

# STATION-WAGON ROAD TRIP

Mom and Dad in the front seat of the car
   Sisters lounging in the backseat singing
Music in harmony, taking us far
   Brother and I, sit in the back, laughing
And waving to the traffic and mugging
   Both of our faces pressed against the glass
Thinking we were cute, but we had no class
   We were just kids on a drive to the shore
Excited, full of energy and sass
   Just sitting in the back, right there on the floor.

# SATURDAY MORNING VOLLEY

Into the coffeehouse the girls stormed
young teens, half a dozen
all wearing sports jerseys and long dark leggings
ponytails high on their heads
strands of hair secured by stretchy headbands.
Each ordered a fancy frozen coffee with
whipped cream piled high
they sat sipping through long green straws
chattering in whispers
while their random giggles became a descant
to the mellow music piped overhead
They delighted in their Saturday morning
post-game treat.
When three young guys strolled in
against the sudden soundtrack of silent moments
With a ready-made audience of turning heads,
darting eyes and bright smiles in unison.
One girl giggled at another, garnering attention
like a serve and a volley,
from one group to the other
And thus, the game was on.

# YOUNG MAN
# WITH A MOHAWK

This young man was once a boy
Proof can be seen upon his face
Shadows of innocence have not faded
Nor sweetness yet displaced

He leaves behind his childhood
Seeking where and how he may fit in
Searching inward for some meaning
Deciding that this is where to begin.

He knows it is not enough just to be
The same as everyone else around
He is strong and smart, and not afraid
Nor is he a sheep in the crowd.

A tattoo is illustrated on his skull
The meaning displayed and exposed
by the spikes of his mohawk reaching up
Like fists, such a fierceness disclosed.

This little while, he is fully expressed.
Yet the strength of it cannot erase
the handsome shadows of innocence
not yet faded from his face.

# UP TO NO GOOD

They were up to no good.
I was a fast runner
The boys were fast too.
I cut across the field
To find a safe place
A hiding space
I thought I could outrun them
Those teenage boys.
I soon found that I could not.
They knocked me down.
My glasses went flying
Later, I told myself
It was all my fault.
I should not have run
For I had become the prey,
While they became the predators.
It was all fun and games for them.
They were up to no good.

# THE DARKEST MOMENTS

Such gentle waves dance against my body
Caressing me as I lay floating, facing the sky
The back of my closed eyelids have become
blood red umbrellas against the sun
The cocoon of heat covers me, beating me
Licking every errant drop of water from my skin
While the gulls overhead are calling out
Alive and thriving, oblivious and not caring
that this anvil, this weight of these severed days
without you breathing in this world
is pressed so heavily upon me
that I could roll right over in this very moment
and sink down, down,
breathing in deep gulps of water
just to be near you again
while the water is salty and tastes like my tears
Which is which? I can't tell the difference.
Yet, I will suffer this damn grief,
this painful hollow of missing,
this excruciating sorrow for as long as I live
While the waves just keep dancing
against my body.

# BIG BROTHER BLUES

When we were kids you teased me often
Or demanded that I leave you alone
While I, insistent, kept hanging on, undaunted
Through the icy blizzard of your demeanor
that I made you wear
Until finally I was pushed back
Flat on my ass
Till, with big gulps of air
and great rivers of tears,
I ran to Mama with lamentations
filled with self-righteous indignation
Of your tortuous rejection
Seeking comfort and justice
for the torments of your tyranny
Only to be faced with an unmoving coldness
From unsympathetic ears
And a slightly less frigid air
than the one you gave me.
No quarter to be found,
neither in you, nor in her
Yet I was drawn to you like a moth
You – the light that I followed
You made me laugh, till you made me cry
I wanted your attention
To look where you were looking
To do what you were doing

To laugh at what you were laughing at
But you hated my fluttering wings
To you I was just an incessant bug
A pest – a brat.
And I was.
I was all that,
What else could I be?
You were the air I breathed
And I didn't know how not
To be a brat, a pest, a bug.
Years have since passed
And we both have grown
And life has set us apart
Each to our own
A different hope
A different dream
A different path
And yet when we interact
I smile to think that I still fancy your attention
To look where you are looking
To do what you are doing
To laugh at what you are laughing at
And my wings still flutter about
Because I have always been
And I will always be,
Now and forever,
Your little sister.

# SISTER CUT

Having been born from the same womb,
That tender filament between us,
That bond of blood
and shared familial memories
Now is severed. Cut.
So hastily, so soon.
And you have taken your end with you.
And I want to pout like a petulant child.
For it was one moment that you were here,
And in the next, gone.
I am left scabless and raw as we all are,
Those of us tied to you by filaments,
The bonds of blood and love.
And I cannot mend this wound.
So I lay prostrate, succumbed to just breathing,
While you do not.
I salt my face with tears, and tire my throat
with great lumps of grief.
I question myself and wonder
why I did not know.
Did I not feel the cut the moment it happened?
Was there no tremor of the filament?
No shaking of the bond?
I was blithely unaware
till I was told about you in words
A delayed reaction — after the fact.

A sonic boom to lay me flat.
Now I find myself sucking on the marrow
of the memories we shared.
Extracting every last bit of remembrance
To sharpen my pain and keep you with me,
Even for a fleeting moment.
As everything about you now is precious.
There is so much meaning to everything
The things you did for others,
The things you made by hand.
The jokes you told, the songs you sang.
Your smile, your laugh.
The way you looked
When you looked at your kids.
The way you loved animals and people.
Your sense of right
and your anger at the wrongs.
Even the sad times now are poignant.
The pain you bore, lessons for us all.
So I raise my glass and stand with applause
For the unique and beautiful heart of you.
You may not know it, you may not have felt it,
but Brava!
You made such a difference to me, to us.
I am so very grateful that I knew you
And loved you and that you loved me too.
For this you can be sure, Sister, I will hold you
in my heart forever.

# LA DANSE APACHE

She is weak
Delicate
Fragile
All skin and bones
With hands and knees
Shaking
As she keeps moving
Forward with her walker
Pausing for a moment
To laugh at the cat
Blocking the path
She walks slowly with purpose
Reaching for the chair
She then transforms and becomes
A Parisienne apache dancer
Throwing herself against caution
Down into the seat
With the flair
Of dramatic exhaustion
Smiling through the whimpers
Or perhaps it's a grimace —
As she closes her eyes
And takes a moment
To recover from the challenge
Of everyday living.

# THE FLY CATCHER

In your elder days when you are wise
Your occupation may just change
To someone who now catches flies

Among your friends, you may inspire
Such gaping caverns of older age
As someone who now catches flies

Or sawing wood, you could advise
To friends with whom you do engage
You're someone who now catches flies

Another job one often tries
Is calling hogs; it's all the rage
In your elder days when you are wise

Some other folks are often hired
For moments when the roof is raised
With someone who now catches flies

These jobs indeed often require
The dreaming days of time and age
In your elder days when you are wise
You'll be the one who catches flies

# LEFT ALONE

I could hear her sobbing.
She woke from sleep, afraid.
Afraid she was all alone.
Everyone left! she cried,
They all left her behind.
Holding her, I tried,
To comfort and reassure her.
Telling her, "Oh Mom!
You are not alone, I am here."
She whimpered
And closed her eyes.
I wrapped her in my arms
And laid down by her side
Till she fell back to sleep.

# LOVE AT 90

He
Slowly
Sits brushing
Her silver mane
His wrinkled hands are shaky but gentle
She doesn't remember him anymore
But she can tell
He's someone
Who loves
Her

# THE POLITICIAN SPOKE

My loss
Has been pronounced
He claims that I am less
Lacking value, with no children—
Just cats.

# TEMAJIN

Flying over a ravine
with the skirt of my yellow dress
flapping behind me,
And my hair blowing in the wind,
while glancing up, I saw you there,
Standing on the bluff overlooking
Lake Michigan,
wearing a white shirt and jeans,
looking all bright in the morning sun,
with arms akimbo.
I called your name but you did not hear,
as the wind in my face swallowed my words
And I flew over to get closer,
to get your attention,
but you did not see me
You simply stood looking over the lake
as if you were waiting for something
My eyes fell upon the others behind you,
Your group of friends laughing, chatting,
calling after you, waiting for you, beckoning.
You turned just then and you saw me
as I was floating above you.
I felt your eyes on me, so filled with love,
and I landed and gave you a hug
And you hugged me back so dearly,

I wanted to stay in that moment, but oh no,
I started rising again, and hovered in midair
While you waved up at me
and then you turned back to your friends,
smiling, they patted your back
and walked away, as you disappeared
under a canopy of trees
and I was sad,
Yet, so glad
to have seen you, touched you,
And I took comfort in knowing
that you were in a good place.

# THE WARRIOR VICTORIOUS

A warrior in gleaming full armor white
Stands ready on my soul's verdant field
While the red moon shines
   in the darkest of night.
My hero, with sword and with shield.
Far across my soul's meadow green.
They sit gnawing, clawing, unaware
Of the warrior, unheeded and unseen
By those twin sisters,
   snarling and crouching there.

Then with a swift and mighty force
The warrior cries out as she charges ahead
Raising high her great mighty sword
An attack so fierce, together both bled.
My warrior "Hope" has fought not in vain
As "Despair" and "Depression"
   in victory were slain!

# YOU MAKE ME WONDER
## – a villanelle

You make me wonder what it's all about.
Is this birthing, living, dying, why we came?
There's more to life than living there's no doubt.

The journey of life for each is a personal route.
Though the end for all is always the same.
You make me wonder what it's all about.

The first breath, the last breath, in, then out.
Witnessing this process, this physical game
You make me wonder what it's all about.

Who started this cycle, this in and out?
Is it science, is it God, that's to blame?
There's more to life than living, there's no doubt.

Philosophers and scientists, they all tout
every conjecture that you could name.
There's more to life than living there's no doubt

Life is amazing, I just want to shout!
Such creative destruction within this frame.
You make me wonder what it's all about.
There's more to life than living there's no doubt.

# IN THAT MOMENT

The waves were crashing against the shore.
The wind was lifting my hair.
The sand felt warm beneath my feet.
The birds were calling overhead.
I took a breath of salty sea air.
And in that moment, I was there.

# THE VERGE OF
# TWILIGHT
## - a pantoum

As the sun keeps time with the moon,
Long shadows of the day grow ever near
Cicadas spend their daily chorus in harmony.
Lo, the heat of the day is slowly spent.

Long shadows of the day grow, ever near,
Flocks of birds in a flurry, tag the tree-tops.
Lo, the heat of the day is slowly spent
With hummingbirds and honeybees waltzing.

Flocks of birds in a flurry, tag the tree-tops,
While a tender breeze flirts and skirts about
With hummingbirds and honeybees waltzing
And pink-laced clouds sail purple skies.

While a tender breeze flirts and skirts about,
Cicadas spend their daily chorus in harmony
And pink-laced clouds sail purple skies,
As the sun keeps time with the moon.

# STRIVING

Striving to be beautiful
We use our hard-earned wages
For a visage mutable
To ward off nature's ages.
Those many funds diverted
Toward every effort
Painstakingly exerted
By some qualified expert.
Nary is their attention
To beautify us inside
No cream or no invention
No surgery betide.
No cures give us honesty
No lotions make us noble
No serums for modesty
And no prescriptions global.
Facing nature's penalty
Kindness should be thriving
There's beauty in empathy
For this, we should be striving.

# GEOMETRIC

There is a secret I've learned
About our universe
Some say we are the stuff of stars
And that may well be true
We are also the stuff
Of lines and shapes and angles
Wavelengths and particles
Intersecting light
Sacred geometry
Golden ratios
Quantum mechanics
I learned this during
A ketamine dream
And I was shown the light
I was shown the shapes,
the fractals
the flower of life
the fruit of life
And I learned the beauty of it
Had I known these truths
Oh if only had I known these truths
I might have studied
Geometry & Physics
Had I known then that
We are the stuff of stars
And the world is all
Geometric

# APPETIZERS

Words beaten, mashed together,
kneaded, rolled, and baked
forming this poem to be shared and supped,
like a wafer of communion,
like the breaking of the bread
in the preface of a Sunday dinner,
where everybody said
that was good, but not a meal,
an appetizer served
as a promise, a hint,
in anticipation of something more
something deeper and more savory yet to come
from somewhere else on the menu
where the entrées can be found.
Sometimes though, we just want the appetizers.

# LOST IN THOUGHT

Here I am in the gray light
as the day gives way to twilight
with an epiphany like a secret lurking
within my mind
hiding itself from view with only its shadows
offering momentary glimpses
of that which I seem to not know
teasing me, taunting me, trying to command me
to find it now, to capture this impression
to reel in this thought not fully formed,
nor fully comprehended.
Aye. It is lost, I cannot capture it.
This thought has dissolved away
like many a dream upon waking,
becoming unrecognizable.
Perhaps it'll reappear
within shadowless display
while I am focused somewhere else,
and quite distracted from this fray.

# A PROMISE OF ANOTHER JOURNEY

I take a step closer and stop
among the pots of colored blooms
with heady perfumes
in contest, each with the other
displaying and creating
their own harmony
seemingly breathing
and vying the attention
of no one in particular
except themselves
and perhaps the one
who set them there.

I take a step closer and I move
on toward great open circles of iron
cast in perfect symmetry,
connected — each with the other
an ornamental portal
of black filigree eternally
striving in vain to claim
a hard, cold, and bold stance
as the guardian of all that lies
within and without.

I take a step closer and I peer
beyond the portal to the other side
where light and shadows dance,
muted — each with the other
by the gauze of the heady perfume
from the blooms on the
other side pervading my senses
and only alabaster stairs
can be somewhat discerned,
each step leading onward
and upward to everything
still unseen,
a promise unspoken,
a promise of another journey.

# IN ONE GLORIOUS CRY

Across the sky, we all can see the moon
amidst a sea of stars, it travels high
so full and round this circular festoon
leaves us bound together in one great sigh
All lunar stages shine unless it's new
for then the night is darkest without light
only the stars in heaven come to view
without the moon, the stars appear so bright
It's knowing we shall see it shine once more
from every single corner of our earth
that gives us comfort in its cycled shore
as we small humans know the moon's full girth
In all applause of shared existence let us try
to praise the moon with one glorious cry.

# THE GENTLE CONFRONTATION

There is a gentle confrontation
when one begins to create
That nudges with excitement
an expression truly great.

There runs a risk, a bit of doubt
that crosses o'er the mind,
It is in the beginning
that commitment lags behind.

When one begins to hesitate,
brush or pen will circle the air,
Before you find the will
to stand and act on what you dare.

Then suddenly a surge of nerves
comes and takes you by the hand,
And courage leads you onward
to take this mighty stand.

`Tis in this possibility
of expression pure and free
Of being known and laying bare
your soul for all to see.

Once that stand is taken
and one begins to create,
It's something out of nothing
that becomes something so great.

It's not in what the critics say
rather it's all in being true
To create an expression
that shows the soul of you.

So take it on – express yourself
and do not hesitate
For in doing so, you just may
inspire others to create!

## 《 INSPIRATION 》

<u>DRIVEL POEM</u>

A poem by my
late sister, Audrey

Yeah tho I walk through the valley
I can't listen to any more drivel
Drivel drives me crazy
Drivel drones in my ear
Drivel is so dramatic
It drains my last drop of energy
I'm drowning in drivel
I am the dromedary in a dry desert
Where sand drives along in the wind
& drills under my skin
Wind driven drivel
Drumming in the distance
As if it were important
But really isn't worth a drachma
Is it my dharma to dance
Through life to drivel waltzes
When I die will they drape me
In a drivel shroud
And drivel flowers all over my coffin
Don't we realize yet
That life and death, these words are
nothing but drivel
Whisper not your dreadful drivel in my ear
But delve with me beyond
Beyond truth
For what is truth but
Brightly polished drivel
To capture our imagination
And how often has the search for truth
Led you to dance to its drivelish humor
And what's all this ecological drivel
And how very bad the bad guys are.
What about napalm
And the atom-splitting holocaust bomb
It took a drooling drivel freak to think those up
And porpoises and whales
How much more drivel can they take
Before splitting this drivel driven planet
For something less noisy
Drop everything
Dump your drivel
Douse it with kerosene & watch it depart
In smoke
The haze that remains is the veil of Isis.

*She's playing
with words
while
diving deep.*

*Wow!*

*Such self-expression!*

--Audrey Yoeckel